Praise for the Believe Series

"As grandparents of fifty grandchildren, we heartily endorse the *Believe and You're There* series. Parents and grandparents, gather your children around you and discover the scriptures again as they come alive in the *Believe and You're There* series."

—STEPHEN AND SANDRA COVEY
Stephen Covey is the bestselling author of *7 Habits of Highly Effective People*

"Bravo! This series is a treasure! You pray that your children will fall in love with and get lost in the scriptures just as they are discovering the wonder of reading. This series does it. Two thumbs way, way up!"

—MACK AND REBECCA WILBERG
Mack Wilberg is the music director of the Mormon Tabernacle Choir

"This series is a powerful tool for helping children learn to liken the scriptures to themselves. Helping children experience the scriptural stories from their point of view is genius."

—ED AND PATRICIA PINEGAR
Ed Pinegar is the bestselling author of *Raising the Bar*

"We only wish these wonderful books had been available when we were raising our own children. How we look forward to sharing them with all our grandchildren!"

—STEPHEN AND JANET ROBINSON
Stephen Robinson is the bestselling author of *Believing Christ*

"The *Believe and You're There* series taps into the popular genre of fantasy and imagination in a wonderful way. Today's children will be drawn into the reality of events described in the scriptures. Ever true to the scriptural accounts, the authors have crafted delightful stories that will surely awaken children's vivid imaginations while teaching truths that will often sound familiar."

—TRUMAN AND ANN MADSEN
Truman Madsen is the bestselling author of *Joseph Smith, the Prophet*

"My dad and I read *At the Miracles of Jesus* together. First I'd read a chapter, and then he would. Now we're reading the next book. He says he feels the Spirit when we read. So do I."

—CASEY J., age 9

"My mom likes me to read before bed. I used to hate it, but the *Believe* books make reading fun and exciting. And they make you feel good inside, too."

—KADEN T., age 10

"Reading the *Believe* series with my tweens and my teens has been a big spiritual boost in our home—even for me! It always leaves me peaceful and more certain about what I believe."

—GLADYS A., age 43

"I love how Katie, Matthew, and Peter are connected to each other and to their grandma. These stories link children to their families, their ancestors, and on to the Savior. I heartily recommend them for any child, parent, or grandparent."

—ANNE S., age 50
Mother of ten, grandmother of nine (and counting)

When David Slew Goliath

Books in the *Believe and You're There* series

Believe and You're There

When David
Slew Goliath

Book 9

ALICE W. JOHNSON & ALLISON H. WARNER

DESERET
BOOK

Salt Lake City, Utah

Library of Congress Cataloging-in-Publication Data

Johnson, Alice W.
    Believe and you're there when David slew Goliath / Alice W. Johnson and Allison H. Warner ; illustrated by Casey Nelson.
        p. cm.
    Summary: Through their grandma's painting, Katie, Matthew, and Peter are whisked to ancient Palestine where Goliath has challenged the Israelites. As they watch young David bravely face Goliath they learn that if you put your faith in God, anything is possible.
    ISBN 978-1-60641-816-1 (paperbound)
    1. David, King of Israel—Juvenile literature.   2. Goliath (Biblical giant)—Juvenile literature.   3. Bible stories, English.   I. Warner, Allison H.
II. Nelson, Casey (Casey Shane), 1973– ill.   III. Title.
    BS580.D3J573 2010
    222'.4—dc22   2010024121

Printed in the United States of America
R. R. Donnelley and Sons, Crawfordsville, IN   10/2010
10   9   8   7   6   5   4   3   2   1

Believe in the wonder,
Believe if you dare,
Believe in your heart,
Just believe . . . and you're there!

Contents

Chapter One

Smooth Stones and Times Tables

After a long, dreary winter, spring had finally arrived! Crocuses pushed their way out of the soft dirt, creating colorful blankets of blooms that hovered just above the ground. Overhead, tender, new foliage shimmered in the sunlight on some trees, with clouds of fresh blossoms clinging to the branches of others.

After being cooped up inside all winter, this was just the kind of day that was perfect for walking to Grandma's house. Grandma had called yesterday to invite her grandchildren to see her newest scripture painting.

And so, on this beautiful Saturday morning, thirteen-year-old Katie and her younger brother, Matthew, led the way along the tree-lined sidewalks, filled with eager anticipation. Eight-year-old Peter shuffled slowly behind, obviously feeling blue.

"What's the matter with him?" Matthew asked Katie quietly. "He sure doesn't seem to be himself today."

It was true. Usually, plucky Peter bounded boisterously ahead of the other children, especially when they were on their way to Grandma's house. But today, he trudged behind, his eyes cast down and his shoulders slumped.

Katie doubled back and slipped her arm around her brother's shoulders. "Hey, buddy, why are you so glum today?"

"Oh, it's nothing," he replied, and kept right on trudging.

Matthew waited for them to catch up. He walked silently beside them for a minute, before asking, "Peter, is something bothering you? Because if there is, I'd love to help. I mean, what are brothers for, after all?"

Peter smiled back weakly. "You wouldn't understand," he mumbled dejectedly, and kept on walking.

"We'd like to try. Come on, won't you give us a

chance?" Katie pleaded, sounding genuinely concerned for her little brother.

Peter finally took his eyes off the sidewalk and looked at Katie and Matthew. "All right," he agreed. "I'm a third grader," he began haltingly, "and third graders are supposed to know their times tables."

"You already know your times tables, don't you?" Matthew asked.

"Yeah, I know them. But on timed tests, it takes me longer than everyone else in the class to write the answers, and sometimes I can't finish them before the time is up," he lamented. "So everyone thinks I am dumb."

"Well, you're definitely not dumb, that's for sure," Matthew said, feeling empathy for his brother's predicament.

"Thanks," Peter replied gratefully. "I'll give you an example of what I mean. On the last timed test, I didn't finish all the problems. But I got all my answers right."

"That's great!" Matthew said.

"Yeah, but I got a lower score than my friend. He finished all the problems, but he got lots of answers wrong," he explained.

"So you are good at math, but you just can't do it fast, is that it?" Katie asked, trying to console him.

Peter nodded and went on, "You know what makes it even worse? My teacher keeps our scores on a chart in the front of the classroom. It is so embarrassing to have everyone know how you're doing. I just can't seem to get any faster," he moaned.

It made Katie sad to see happy-go-lucky Peter so discouraged. "Don't worry, we'll think of something," she said, reassuring him as she patted his mop of red-brown curls affectionately.

In return, Peter gave his sister one of his big signature bear hugs. "Hey, let's take the shortcut through the park," he said enthusiastically as he took off in a trot, with Matthew following close behind. A trip through the park was always fun and, for the moment, he felt a little better.

The pond in the middle of the park was the perfect place for skipping stones. By the time Katie reached the boys, they each had a collection of smooth, flat stones stuffed in their pockets. They stood side by side at the water's edge, skipping the stones across the glassy surface of the pond. The skip of the stones made a patchwork of circular ripples that disappeared into soft waves, lapping gently at the shore.

Peter sent a smooth stone skipping six times along the water. "Wow, six times! I think that's my record," he declared proudly.

Matthew tried to beat Peter's record, but he was having no luck. He gave it one more try, but he didn't even come close. "You've got me totally beat, little brother," he confessed reluctantly.

"I'll give you one more chance," Peter offered.

"I'm all out of stones," Matthew said. "And besides, you'd still beat me. You're the best!"

"At least I'm good at something, even if I can't

do math as fast as other kids can," Peter said, remembering the difficulty that still faced him.

"Hey! You're good at lots of things," Matthew said. "For one thing, you always win when we play checkers."

Katie, who had been watching the family of ducks that made its home on the banks of the pond, noticed the sun was now high overhead. Time was slipping away. "Uh-oh, guys! I think we'd better hurry along to Grandma's house," Katie reminded them as she watched the ducklings fall in line behind their mother and parade around the pond. "You never know what exciting adventures are in store for us today."

"I almost forgot!" Peter said with genuine enthusiasm.

"We lost track of the time, didn't we?" Matthew remarked, checking his watch. "Let's get going!" he called over his shoulder as he took off running across the park. Katie and Peter followed behind him, and the three siblings looked a little like the family of ducks at the pond.

"I hope we're not too late," Peter panted, trying to catch his breath.

"Me, too," Matthew wheezed.

"Please, can't we slow down a little?" Katie begged her brothers as she fell farther and farther behind.

"Oh, all right," Matthew said, taking pity on his sister in her wedged sandals. "I just can't wait to get there."

So far, each of Grandma's special paintings had come alive—literally—as Grandma read aloud the scripture story the painting depicted. And then, each painting had carried the children back in time to experience the scriptures for themselves!

Each picture Grandma painted for them had these magical qualities, and the children hadn't yet been disappointed. But each time they visited Grandma, they wondered: Will the scripture adventures continue? Will the magic last?

Chapter Two

Feeling "Upsad"

Grandma sat patiently, watching for the children, swinging gently in her front porch swing, and basking in the beautiful spring morning.

As always, she eagerly anticipated her grandchildren's arrival. How she loved sharing the scriptures with them! And today, she felt in her heart that she had chosen just the right story.

Finally, she saw them round the corner and bound down the street. She waved a happy hello. The children, seeing the welcoming face of their beloved grandma, raced to her porch and fell in a heap, trying to catch their breath.

"What fun have you kids been up to now?" Grandma asked, laughing at her energetic grandchildren.

"We decided to walk to your house because the day is so beautiful," Katie told her breathlessly.

"Then we took the shortcut through the park," Matthew continued.

"But it wasn't really much of a shortcut, because we stopped at the pond and skipped rocks," Peter informed her when his panting slowed. "I beat my own record skipping rocks. I found the perfect stone, and it skipped six times across the water."

"Six times? That's impressive! You'll have to give me a demonstration someday," Grandma said admiringly.

"He sure is good at skipping rocks. He beats me almost every time we skip," Matthew offered, complimenting his little brother.

Suddenly, Peter's face fell, and the gloom he felt earlier descended like a dark cloud. "At least I'm good at something!" he said dejectedly.

"What's troubling you, Peter?" Grandma asked.

Peter let out a long, heavy sigh and began, "I'm really having trouble with times tables. I'm not nearly as fast at them as most other kids in the third grade. It makes me feel dumb, and I think I'm depressed about it," he confessed.

"What do you mean by depressed?" Grandma asked him gently.

"Don't you know what depressed means, Grandma?" Peter asked.

"Well, I know what it means to me. I was just wondering what it means to you," she coaxed him, looking a bit amused.

"It means you're down in the dumps. It's like being upset and sad at the same time. I call it 'upsad,'" Peter explained, sounding like a professor.

Grandma smiled down at her grandson, impressed by his observations. "You just made up a brand new word! That definitely requires some smarts. *Upsad.* I like that word! I'm going to use it a lot."

"That doesn't solve my problem with math though," Peter said, still sounding discouraged.

"Just because things are hard doesn't mean there isn't a way to conquer them," Grandma said, trying to sound upbeat.

"Yeah, but this problem is so big, Grandma." Peter turned down his lips in a definite pout.

"Hmm, I see," she said, pretending to be deep in thought, but her eyes danced with a certain sparkle. "I think I may have something that could help."

Katie recognized that sparkle, and her stomach filled with butterflies. She felt a trip to the art cottage was about to happen, and she looked with anticipation at Grandma's face.

Matthew felt it too, and he held his breath until Grandma pushed herself up and out of the swing, cheerily announcing, "Let's make a little visit to the art cottage, shall we?"

A trip to the art cottage made even Peter forget his troubles, and he was the first one in line to lead the procession. Grandma's backyard was in full bloom, and the magical art cottage was nestled in thick clusters of pink and white petunias, while rows of red and yellow tulips lined the winding flagstone path that led to its blue arched door.

Peter stopped on the porch of the little cottage and waited for his cue. "Go ahead," Grandma said, passing him the key.

Taking his job very seriously, Peter stood at attention, holding the key aloft. With great ceremony, and in his best British accent, he began the

11

verse they all knew by heart. "Believe," he uttered, with great formality.

"In the wonder," Matthew, Katie, and Grandma said together.

"Believe," Peter went on.

"If you dare," came the response.

"Believe," Peter kept the poem going.

"In your heart!"

"Just believe," Peter said, his voice rising in crescendo as he set up the big finish.

"And you're there!" they all shouted in rousing chorus.

Peter turned the key in the lock and bowed grandly. "My ladies," he said, beckoning Grandma and Katie to enter.

Giggling, they walked through the blue door, stopping on the way to curtsy to Peter.

Peter bowed again and invited Matthew with a stately, "My lord."

Matthew returned the bow and entered the cottage. Peter followed closely behind.

Grandma took her place in her rocking chair, and the three hopeful children perched on the floor pillows. The easel stood before them, draped

in a white sheet, with the corners of the mystery painting's frame poking out on either side.

"Peter, this painting is for you," Grandma announced. "I didn't know it was for you when I painted it, but I know now. So, why don't you be the one to remove the drape?"

At her invitation, Peter jumped up and pulled the drape off the easel with a royal flourish. On the canvas, Grandma had painted a valley, bordered by mountains on its left and right. A narrow stream ran the length of the valley floor between the mountains on either side, dividing the valley into two distinct halves. Short, shady trees were scattered along the water's path. On either side of the valley were two large encampments in the foothills of the mountains.

In the middle of the valley, standing on one side of the trickling water and facing the other side, stood a giant of a man, a huge brass helmet on his head. His massive upper body was covered with a heavy coat of armor.

In contrast, on the other side of the stream, facing the giant straight on, was a young boy. He looked to be about Matthew's size. Dressed in only a simple tunic, with a shepherd's bag slung across his shoulder, he held a slingshot ready in one hand and a shepherd's staff in the other.

Peter instantly recognized the scene and announced with confidence, "Hey! That's David and Goliath!"

Chapter Three

Off to War

"Exactly!" Grandma beamed at Peter. "What a smart young man you are, my boy. This is David, who went down into the valley of Elah to do battle with the giant Philistine named Goliath."

"What valley did you say it was?" Matthew asked.

"The valley of Elah. It is named for the Elah trees that you see in the valley and on the mountains," Grandma said.

"David looks so small compared to Goliath," Peter observed as he studied the painting carefully. "It seems impossible that a kid that small could win a battle with that big, huge man."

"Well, it was impossible, except for one thing:

David had God on his side," Grandma pointed out.

"Right! I learned a scripture that says, 'For with God nothing shall be impossible,'" Katie recalled.

"Nothing, except for math," Peter moaned.

"Everyone has to confront big problems, Peter. Some people say it this way: 'We all have our Goliaths to face,'" Grandma told her young grandson.

Peter screwed up his face and gave Grandma a quizzical look.

"What she's trying to say is that some problems seem as big to us as Goliath must have seemed to David," Matthew explained.

"Oh, I get it," said Peter, the light going on. "You're talking about how that little piece of paper filled with times tables—you know, the one we use to take timed tests—seems at least as hard to face as facing Goliath would be."

"Right!" Grandma nodded enthusiastically. "Now, let's get to the story, and I think you'll see even better just what I'm talking about." And with that, she lifted her worn Bible onto her lap, positioning her reading glasses on the tip of her nose.

Peter felt his heart beat a little faster at the prospect of a new adventure, and so he sat very still (an unusual occurrence), waiting for Grandma to begin.

"I think I had better give you a little background before we jump into the story. Does anyone know anything about David's life before he faced Goliath?" Grandma asked, curious to learn how much the children knew. She was about to be pleasantly surprised.

"Where should we start?" Katie asked.

"Start with what you know," Grandma prompted.

"Well, for one thing, David was a shepherd," Katie began.

"And he played a harp and made up a lot of songs for his sheep," Peter said.

Grandma laughed at Peter's creativity. "The scriptures tell us he played the harp," she confirmed. "We definitely know that much."

"And he was anointed to become king," Matthew added.

"And he lived in Bethlehem, the same city where Jesus was born," Peter pointed out.

"Right! The scriptures even call Bethlehem 'the city of David,'" Grandma said. "And they prophesy that Jesus would come out of the stem of Jesse."

"What does 'the stem of Jesse' mean?" Katie asked.

"That's a good question. Jesse was David's father, and it was through his lineage, or in other words, through his descendants, that Mary, Jesus' mother, was born. And through her, Jesus came into the world," Grandma explained. "You kids seem to know a lot about David, don't you? Why don't we fill in the rest by reading the story from the Bible?"

Immediately, her three grandchildren snapped to attention and sat like statues, hardly breathing, ready for a trip to the valley of Elah.

Seemingly unaware of the children's anxiousness, Grandma picked up her Bible and leafed through its pages to find her place.

"Here we go," she said at last, and she began reading. "'And Saul and the men of Israel were gathered together, and pitched by the valley of Elah, . . . And the Philistines stood on a mountain on the one side, and Israel stood on a mountain on the other side. . . . And there went out a champion out of the camp of the Philistines, named Goliath, of Gath, whose height was six cubits and a span.' Scholars say that's probably over nine feet tall, children," Grandma interjected.

As she spoke, three pairs of eyes were riveted to the painting on the easel, searching for even the slightest sign of movement. Then, suddenly, there it was! In the painting, Goliath stepped forward to face the Israelites, and he raised his spear high in the air.

Peter was the first to detect the movement. He elbowed both Katie and Matthew in the ribs. "Come on, let's go!" he whispered.

"Okay!" Matthew offered Peter his hand, ready for a new escapade.

"Uh, hold on, guys," Katie whispered. "I'm not so sure about this. What happens if those armies start fighting while we're there?"

"We'll stick together so we can come home any time we want," Peter assured her in hushed tones. But Katie was still unconvinced.

"Don't worry, Sis. We'll protect you," Matthew added in a low murmur so Grandma wouldn't hear.

Reassured by Matthew's promise, Katie locked hands with Peter, held her breath, and closed her eyes in anticipation of their departure. Then Matthew pushed his free hand into the canvas of the painting, right near the Israelite encampment. Matthew's hand seemed to be swallowed up by the painting's landscape. Then his arm, his shoulder, and his whole body disappeared. And, in a moment, Katie and Peter, linked to Matthew by their clasped hands, were sucked in too. The wind rushed by, swirling around them. WHOOSH! The children were airborne. Behind them lay the safety and security of the art cottage. Before them lay the valley of Elah, where the Philistines and the Israelites faced each other, prepared to do battle.

The children skimmed the branches of the Elah trees as the air that kept them aloft slowed and deposited them softly in the shade. When Katie opened her eyes, she let out a grateful sigh, relieved that they were safely tucked out of sight behind the trunk of a tree.

"Yahoo! I love that part!" Peter exclaimed, and then broke out into uncontrollable laughter. "Matthew, look at you! Nice dress!"

Matthew looked down at his attire, and said, "And I don't love this part. But at least we're in the same boat. You look as funny as I do, bro."

Each boy was dressed in a loosely woven tunic, with a geometric design painted around the edge of its hem. A large piece of animal skin was draped diagonally across each boy's body, from shoulder to knee. The whole outfit was belted at the waist with a narrow leather sash. A small pouch hung from each belt, and sturdy leather sandals protected the children's feet from the dry, rocky ground.

"I think I look good in my dress," Katie said, admiring her long, loose tunic. A pretty purple sash wrapped around her waist, and her blonde hair was tucked safely underneath a traditional protective head scarf.

Satisfied that there was nothing about them that would give away their true identities, the three children ventured out from behind the tree to find themselves right at the edge of the Israelite encampment.

Chapter Four

Fast Friends

The Israelite camp consisted of a sea of make-shift tents spread across the low rise of foothills now before the children. The sprawling encampment lay just below a range of imposing mountains and just above the valley floor. Crude animal stalls had been erected around the outer edges of the camp. Here, the Israelite soldiers kept an assortment of horses, goats, and sheep.

From their landing spot, the children could see a narrow dirt path that led past the animal stalls and disappeared into the camp.

"Let's follow that path," Peter suggested, eager to explore.

"Under one condition, Peter," Katie instructed.

"We all must stay together until we're sure we are safe here."

"Okay, I can agree to that," Peter promised, raising his right hand as if he were making a solemn oath.

"It looks pretty safe from here," Matthew said, looking over the encampment and the valley below.

The three latter-day children scrambled over and around the rocky terrain until they reached the narrow dirt path. Cautiously, they started toward the camp. They had taken only a few steps on the path when they heard footsteps approaching from behind.

"Where are you going?" a boy's voice demanded. "Are you Philistine spies?"

The children froze in their tracks. Katie grabbed Matthew's hand and began feeling around frantically for Peter's, but she couldn't find it.

"Why are you here?" a girl's voice, full of suspicion, asked next.

Slowly, the children turned around, and a wave of relief washed over them. On the path behind them stood a boy and a girl just about Matthew's age.

"We're not spies, I promise. We are visiting this valley, and we're headed right over there." Peter pointed in the direction of the camp.

"That is where we are going too," said the dark-haired girl, smiling now that she knew that Katie, Matthew, and Peter meant no harm to the Israelites. "We are bringing provisions to our brother." She held aloft the basket she was carrying.

"Do you have family in the army too?" the boy asked.

"No, we're here all by ourselves," Matthew answered, hoping the questions wouldn't keep coming.

"Well, then," the boy said brightly, to Matthew's relief, "my name is Samuel, and this is my sister, Susannah."

"I am Peter. We're siblings, and I'm the youngest," Peter greeted them. "This is my older brother, Matthew, and my sister, Katie, the oldest."

Peter looked back and forth from Samuel to Susannah several times with a puzzled look on his face. "I can't tell. Which one of you is older?"

"Neither one of us," Samuel answered. "We're twins."

"Actually, I am older by a few minutes," Susannah teased.

"And she never lets me forget it." Samuel laughed good-naturedly.

Susannah took Katie's hand and smiled. "Hello, Katie. I am very glad to meet you. I was afraid I would be the only girl in the camp."

"I was worried about that too," Katie admitted, "but now that you're here, I feel so much better." Katie returned Susannah's welcoming smile.

"Why don't you come with us to visit our older brother, Ethan? He is camped here with the army. Our parents have sent us to check on him and to bring him food and supplies."

"We'd like that," Matthew said, readily accepting their offer.

"Come, then," Samuel said as he linked arms with Matthew and Peter. The five fast friends confidently marched into the camp.

"I have never been to a battlefield before. I'm a little frightened to be here," Katie confessed to Susannah when the boys were out of earshot.

"I was a little concerned too, Katie," Susannah assured her. "But the battle has not yet begun, and so my parents agreed to let me come with Samuel. And besides, my older brother can protect us."

Following the boys, they entered the camp through an opening between the tents that was guarded by an Israelite soldier. He recognized the twins.

"Hello, Samuel and Susannah. You must be bringing provisions for Ethan. My children have

not come for ten days now, but I expect them to-day," he said, eyeing the basket hungrily.

Susannah smiled. "Well, we cannot have you faint from lack of food, can we?" She reached into the basket and pulled out some dried figs and a handful of almonds. "Will that be enough until your children come?" she inquired, depositing the food in the guard's outstretched hand.

"Thank you, children," he said gratefully. "I will eat these one at a time to make them last. I think Ethan is in his tent right now. He will be

very glad to see you." The children left the guard munching happily on the almonds and figs.

The wide paths running through the encampment were filled with soldiers, all of them waiting for the day when the battle would begin. Some slept under their tents, others sat huddled in earnest conversations, and still others sharpened spears and swords in preparation for battle.

Peter gawked, fascinated by the bundles of spears stacked at each tent door. "Wow, look at all those spears. I've never seen so many weapons in one place before."

"They are everywhere. I'm sure Ethan will let you hold his when we get to his tent," Samuel said.

"Really? Let's hurry then!" Peter's whole face lit up, excited by the thought.

As they rounded the next corner, zigzagging through the endless tents, a boy who appeared to be just older than Katie was walking toward them. He, too, carried a basket filled with food. Peter noticed that the boy had a small pouch just like the one in his own belt, and that the boy carried a shepherd's hooked staff. He smiled as he passed, and Samuel and Susannah waved and nodded to him.

"Who is that?" Matthew asked.

"That is a shepherd boy named David. He sometimes comes to bring his brothers food and provisions, just like we do. And," Susannah spoke importantly, "he is anointed to become king one day."

"He looks so ordinary," Katie remarked.

"I think we are all pretty ordinary, until we answer God's call to do His work," Samuel spoke thoughtfully, but with authority.

"Samuel! Susannah!"

"Ethan!" Susannah cried, and ran into her brother's outstretched arms. She squealed with delight as the young man swung her around, lifting her high in the air. He set her down softly, and then he and Samuel clasped each other by the forearm, and pulled each other into a long, brotherly embrace.

"I didn't know you two were coming today," Ethan said, clearly delighted by the unexpected visit.

"Mother and Father were anxious to know how you were," Samuel explained.

"And, of course, Mother was worried that you didn't have enough to eat," Susannah said, producing the basket brimming with food.

"What a welcome surprise," Ethan said, eagerly examining the contents of the basket. "My favorite twins and Mother's cooking! Who could ask for more?"

Chapter Five

For Who Can Slay the Giant?

Ethan set the basket of food on a flat rock in front of his tent. He pulled out a fresh round loaf of bread and tore off a piece for each of the children.

"You are welcome to share my bread, but don't you think I ought to know your names first?" he asked the three unfamiliar children with a wink.

"I completely forgot!" Samuel exclaimed. "Ethan, these are our new friends, Matthew, Katie, and Peter."

"I am happy to meet you," Ethan replied warmly. "What brings you to the valley of Elah?"

"We heard about the giant, Goliath, and we're hoping to see him. Have you ever seen him?" Peter asked, hardly able to contain his excitement.

"Oh yes, many times," Ethan said.

"What does he look like?" Peter's eyes were as big as saucers. "Is he really as big as they say he is?"

"He surely is the largest man I have ever seen," Ethan began. "He is six cubits and a span." Ethan held his arm up as high as it could go to indicate Goliath's height.

Matthew reminded Peter quietly, "Remember, Grandma said that he is over nine feet tall."

Peter's mouth dropped open. "He really is a giant, isn't he?"

"It is hard to believe, isn't it?" Ethan responded.

"Does he have a spear?" Peter's questions kept coming. "'Cause I'm really interested in weapons."

"Oh yes, his spear is twice as big as mine. It makes mine look like a child's toy," Ethan said, pointing to his own large spear resting against his tent.

A commotion rippled through the camp, and a cry went up. "Goliath is coming to challenge us," the Israelites shouted to each other. "Goliath is coming again!" The soldiers in the camp hurried to the edge of the hill to see the giant striding to the center of the valley below.

"Come on, let's go!" Peter urged impatiently.

"May we go too?" Samuel asked Ethan.

"Yes, you children may go. But let us stay close together," Ethan instructed.

The boys leapt to their feet, but Katie and Susannah hung back, a wave of panic gripping them.

Sensing their distress, Ethan took the girls aside, placing his hands reassuringly on their shoulders. "Goliath is down in the center of the valley, while we are up in the foothills. He is probably planning just to issue his challenge again, as he has every day for some weeks now. We will be safe here. Come, you may each take one of my hands. We shall go together."

Reassured by Ethan's words, Katie and Susannah each grabbed one of his strong hands, and they all followed the crowd of soldiers toward the edge of the foothill.

When they reached the hill's brow, they saw two men from the Philistine army advance across the valley floor toward the Israelite camp. A shield bearer led the way, dwarfed by the menacing Goliath, who followed behind him.

Goliath looked fearsome, dressed from head to

toe in full battle armor. He had a helmet of brass upon his head, revealing only his face and forehead, and his midsection was protected by a coat of mail. His shins were covered with armor, and a metal shield stretched between his shoulders to protect his neck. In his hand, he carried a gigantic spear, its sharpened tip glistening in the noonday sunlight.

The shield bearer and the giant stopped on the banks of the stream. Goliath spread his feet wide and planted them firmly, facing the Israelite encampment. And then he dramatically thrust his spear into the ground.

From this position he issued his daily challenge to the Israelite army:

"Choose you a man for you, and let him come down to me. If he be able to fight with me, and to kill me, then will we be your servants: but if I prevail against him, and kill him, then shall ye be our servants, and serve us."

There was no answer from the Israelite camp.

"What is the Israelite army going to do?" Peter asked Ethan.

"No one knows what to do. There is not one

Israelite who can compare to Goliath in size or strength. If we send a man to do battle with him, he will surely die," Ethan said.

"And then we will be the servants of the Philistines. I do not want that to happen," Samuel added.

"Neither does anyone else. But who can slay the giant?" Ethan asked, as the huge Philistine swaggered defiantly back and forth on the battlefield.

Goliath waited for a response. When no answer came, Goliath plucked his spear out of the ground, held it high above his head and bellowed, "I defy the armies of Israel this day; give me a man, that we may fight together."

Dismayed and frightened by the giant's demands, the Israelites remained silent.

Finally, Goliath threw back his head and laughed scornfully, mocking the cowardly Israelite army. His loud guffaws echoed across the enclosed valley. Then he turned his back on the Israelites and strode triumphantly up the hill to the Philistine camp.

"Thank goodness he's gone!" Katie shuddered, watching Goliath thunder across the valley.

"He is gone for now, but he will return later today," Ethan told her.

"He is coming again? Are you sure? Then let us go quickly," Susannah said, turning back toward the camp.

"How do you know he will come back?" Katie asked Ethan.

"Each day, for the last forty days, Goliath has issued that same challenge, both morning and night," Ethan explained. "Of course, no one has yet accepted."

"Can you blame them?" Peter asked.

"Oh no, I don't blame them. I don't want to fight Goliath, either, but this confrontation cannot go on forever," Ethan said.

"Then how it will end?" Matthew asked.

"I wish I knew." Ethan shook his head despondently.

"Can the king do something about it?" Samuel asked.

"I am afraid the king is as frightened as the rest of us are," Ethan replied. He shook his head one last time.

"I wish I were big. I would fight him for sure," Peter declared boldly.

"You're just itching to get your hands on one of those spears, aren't you, buddy?" Matthew teased.

"How did you know?" Peter asked, smiling sheepishly.

"I know you really well, that's how," Matthew said.

"Peter, did you see the spears at my tent?" Ethan asked.

Peter answered by nodding his head.

"Well, the first one of you boys to reach the tent can try one of them," Ethan promised with a chuckle.

Samuel and Matthew didn't even have a chance. Peter was just too fast for either of them. By the time they caught up with him, he was at the door of Ethan's tent, standing at attention, and holding Ethan's spear at attention too.

Chapter Six

Is There Not a Cause?

By the end of the afternoon, with Ethan's help, Peter had become surprisingly proficient with the spear. Holding it above his shoulder, right next to his ear, he ran through the rolling fields behind the sea of tents and pumped the spear up into the sky. It sailed, unwavering, through the air, until its tip nudged downward, and it plunged securely into the ground.

"Peter, you are quite the spear thrower. Many soldiers cannot throw a spear as well as you can," Ethan complimented the boy sincerely.

Peter beamed and ran to retrieve the weapon.

Katie and Susannah spent the afternoon gathering wildflowers on the grassy hills behind the camp. They sat happily under an Elah tree, weaving colorful blossoms into long garlands, which they fashioned into rainbow-hued necklaces, bracelets, and beautiful flower crowns.

Matthew and Samuel took their turns throwing the spear, but neither could match Peter's uncanny skill. When they were all worn out, Ethan and the boys joined Katie and Susannah under the tree.

"You two girls look lovely," Ethan said, admiring their handiwork.

"Thank you," they answered in unison, delighted by Ethan's praise.

"When will Goliath come out again? I don't want to miss him," Peter said, plopping himself on the ground next to Ethan.

"He shall come very soon, I would say, judging by the position of the sun. Let us go see what is happening in the camp," Ethan suggested, standing up and stretching in the afternoon sun.

"May I carry your spear?" Peter asked.

"Certainly, Peter. You have earned the privilege of being our spear bearer and leading us back to camp," Ethan declared, handing Peter the spear with a ceremonial bow.

Ethan and the others lined up behind Peter,

who triumphantly led the parade back into the camp.

Just as the procession reached the tents, the cry arose: "Goliath is coming! He is coming!" The entire Israelite camp emptied onto the ridge once more to witness the giant hurling his insults across the valley. Ethan and the children hurried to join the throng gathering on the hillside.

"Look, there is David!" Samuel pointed to the young shepherd boy who stood nearby with his oldest brother, Eliab.

All eyes were on Goliath as he strode again to the stream's edge in his cumbersome armor. As before, his shield bearer stood before him, and Goliath positioned himself to roar his daily challenge to the Israelites. Behind him, the Philistine army was arrayed, standing at attention on the hillside opposite the Israelites.

Fear gripped the Israelite soldiers, and many fled back into the camp to escape the giant's menacing proposal. But some remained on the brow of the hill, including Ethan and the children, David the young shepherd boy, and David's brother, Eliab.

One Israelite soldier boldly asked his compatriots, "Who is this man, Goliath, that threatens the army of the living God? Is there no one here willing to defend Israel's honor?"

"Have you seen how big he is? Everyone is afraid of being killed himself, and then we all would become slaves of the Philistines," another soldier attempted to explain.

"I have thought about going against him myself, to reap the rewards offered by King Saul," said another.

"Rewards?" asked young David, who had been listening with great interest.

"King Saul has offered a handsome reward to the man who kills Goliath. Saul has promised to bestow great riches and to give to the victor his own daughter in marriage. And the victor's family will never have to pay taxes again."

"Surely there must be one courageous Israelite who would consider it an honor to fight this giant, not for the king's reward, but to save all Israel," David said.

Eliab laughed at his little brother's confident judgment of the situation. He turned to his

brother and said, "Courage is for warriors, little brother, not for shepherds. Who is taking care of your sheep?"

"My sheep are safe, brother," David replied. "I just don't understand; is there not a cause for one of us to fight the giant?"

Peter and Matthew turned to Ethan, a question on their faces. "A cause?" Peter asked.

Ethan readily interpreted David's question. "Clearly, David believes that when Goliath curses Israel, he also curses God. And defending our God is just cause to slay Goliath. I think David is saying that the man who steps forward to face Goliath will be doing God's will."

After David raised his all-important question, he turned to the others in the crowd, and asked again if there was no man who would defend Israel and its God against the unjustified railings of Goliath.

The answer was unchanged: No man could fight Goliath and win. If the king was unwilling to take on the giant himself, his promised rewards were not enough to convince a single Israelite soldier to lose his life by facing the formidable giant, thus condemning the entire Israelite army to be the servants of the Philistines.

Then David squared his young shoulders, his mind made up. He would not shrink from the challenge made by Goliath. He said to the soldiers gathered around him that he was willing to contend with Goliath himself, trusting that God would deliver him.

Watching David stand taller, proclaiming his determination to meet Goliath himself, the gathered soldiers gasped. The young shepherd boy was going to accept the giant's challenge! Peter's mouth dropped open. In a voice filled with admiration, he said, "But he is so small! That's a lot of courage— and a lot of faith!"

"Do you think there is any way he can bring down Goliath?" Samuel asked Matthew in a low voice.

"He seems to think he can," Matthew answered him.

"But how?" Samuel asked, worried for David.

"I don't know how, but with the Lord on your side you can do amazing things. You can even do things that seem impossible," Matthew said.

"Well, he is going to need all the help he can get, judging from his size and the size of Goliath," Peter said.

At the brow of the hill, David looked out across the valley. Goliath, who still faced the Israelites with brashness and arrogance, was unaware that a young shepherd, filled with faith in God and a desire to serve Him, had determined to defend Israel's honor.

Chapter Seven

The Lord Looketh on the Heart

The news of David's bold questions, and his subsequent determination to answer Goliath's challenge himself, raced through the camp. Soldiers who had witnessed the exchange between David and the soldiers spread the story to those who had fled from the hilltop. Soon the story was on everyone's lips. Astonished by David's decision, a group of men hurried to King Saul's tent to tell him what had transpired.

Ethan gathered the children and took them back to his tent. "I was very worried out there," he said, shaking his head. "Since no one has yet answered Goliath's challenge, I was afraid the Philistines would attack us, and we would have been in the middle of a fierce battle. What would I have told Mother and Father if anything had happened to you?"

"You mean we would have seen the soldiers use their spears?" Peter asked eagerly.

"Yes, you would have seen lots of spears. But trust me, Peter, you would not have liked it. No one in his right mind wants to go to war, ever," Ethan's tone was grim, his dislike for war showing on his face.

"I've only seen it in the movies," Peter admitted.

"The what?" Samuel was puzzled.

"You know, movies—" Peter began to explain.

"Don't you mean murals, Peter? You've only seen pictures of war on murals," Matthew prompted him.

"Murals! How right you are!" Peter agreed, catching on to his mistake.

Ethan disappeared into his tent and returned with the large basket of food the twins had brought. "Let's have something to eat, shall we?"

Ethan and all five children sat together on the ground in front of Ethan's tent. He tore pieces of bread from a round loaf and passed one to each person.

"How did David ever find the courage to volunteer to fight Goliath?" Katie asked Ethan.

"David is a remarkable young man. When he was young, he was anointed to become the king of Israel someday. Since then, I have always felt that he has a special mission to perform. Perhaps facing Goliath is part of that mission."

"Who chose him to be the future king? And why wasn't Eliab chosen, since he is the oldest son?" Peter asked.

"The Lord sent Samuel to visit David's father, Jesse—" Ethan began.

"He sent you?" Matthew looked right at Samuel, Susannah's twin.

Samuel laughed. "No, not me. Samuel the prophet."

"Oh, I see," Matthew replied.

"Samuel told Jesse that God had chosen a king from among Jesse's sons. Samuel instructed Jesse to choose a cow to sacrifice and then to go with him to perform the sacrifice. Samuel said that at the appointed place, God would make it known to him whom to anoint." Ethan paused and took a sack of almonds out of the basket, offering a handful to each of the children.

"Go on," Susannah said, munching happily on the nuts.

"At the sacrifice, Samuel first looked at Eliab, Jesse's oldest son, and said, 'Surely the Lord's anointed is before him.' But the Lord said to Samuel, 'Look not on his countenance, or on the height of his stature, . . . I have refused him, . . . for man looketh on the outward appearance, but the Lord looketh on the heart.'"

"Then what happened?" Katie pressed.

"When Jesse had presented seven of his sons to Samuel, the prophet said, 'The Lord hath not chosen these. Are here all thy children?'"

"That is when Jesse told him about David, his youngest son, isn't it?" Susannah said, remembering the story.

"Yes, so Jesse sent for David and when Samuel saw him, the Lord said, 'Arise, anoint him: for this is he.' Then Samuel . . . anointed him in the midst of his brethren: and the Spirit of the Lord came upon David from that day forward."

"No wonder David spoke with such power and confidence today. He knows he can rely on the Lord to help him," Matthew said knowingly.

"I think you are right, Matthew," Ethan said, as he reached into the basket and produced another cloth sack, this one filled with figs. "Here, have some," Ethan offered, passing the sack around. Katie and Matthew had learned to love the sweet, juicy fruit, but Peter still didn't care for all those seeds. He gingerly took the top of the sack with two fingers and quickly passed it on.

Ethan proceeded to explain: "Remember what the Lord promised Abraham? He made a covenant with Father Abraham a long time ago, that whosoever blessed Abraham would be blessed, and whosoever cursed Abraham would be cursed. Goliath has cursed all Israel and the God of Abraham. So David can depend on the covenant to protect him as he defends Israel and our God."

"Even so, he must have a lot of faith to be willing to fight someone as scary as Goliath," Peter observed, a picture of the giant dressed for battle looming in his mind. "God could see David's heart when He chose him as the future king. But now, we all get to see just how brave and true that heart is."

"Samuel, remember the song we learned from

David about trusting in God?" Susannah asked. "David writes songs, you know, and this one surely expresses his amazing faith. Shall we sing it for everyone?"

"Oh yes, we would love to hear it," Katie encouraged them.

Samuel produced a wooden flute from his belt and played a short introduction. Then the Israelite twins began to sing in clear voices that blended perfectly together:

> *Come, sing unto the mighty God of*
> *Israel,*
> *Pray unto Him in faith, and never*
> *cease.*
> *For God doth hear the pleadings of*
> *the righteous,*
> *And blesses them with safety and*
> *with peace.*
> *Our God defends all those who love*
> *and trust Him.*
> *All evil and deceit He doth destroy.*
> *Then let us come into His house of*
> *mercy,*
> *And in His name forever shout for*
> *joy.*

When Samuel and Susannah finished singing, Peter was the first to speak. "If David has faith to face Goliath, then we should have faith that he can win."

"I have faith that he can win, but I wish there were something we could do to help him," Katie said.

"We could pray," Matthew suggested. "We could pray that David will be strengthened and protected as he goes to meet Goliath."

"That is a wonderful idea, Matthew," Ethan said. "Come, children, let us kneel together. Let us pray that the God of Abraham will protect young David, the future king of Israel."

Chapter Eight

"Go, and the Lord Be with Thee"

King Saul sat in his tent, glum and pensive. He feared that if a willing Israelite didn't come forward soon to fight Goliath, his people would begin to wonder why the king (who was very tall and strong) didn't take on the giant himself. This question threatened to destroy Saul's reputation in his kingdom.

As Saul fretted, his chamberlain came to his tent. He approached the brooding king cautiously. "Your Majesty, there are men here who have news for you. They humbly request permission to address you."

Saul nodded, granting the men permission to approach. After all, their news couldn't be worse than what he already faced.

"Your Majesty," one of the men addressed the king, "there is one who has stepped forward to answer Goliath's challenge."

Saul sat up straight in his chair, a glimmer of hope flickering in his eyes. Finally, he thought, an Israelite who is willing to defend our honor.

"Who is this soldier?" the king asked hopefully. "Who is the man that has willingly offered to fight the giant?"

"He is not a man, O king. He is a shepherd boy who came to the camp to visit his brothers," one soldier responded.

"A shepherd boy?" Saul was open-mouthed, stunned. "Bring him here, that I may see him for myself."

The soldiers found David preparing to meet Goliath. "King Saul has summoned you," they informed the boy. "We are to escort you to his tent."

David readily obeyed the king's command, following the soldiers to the waiting king. All eyes were on the boy as he walked through the camp, and murmurs of admiration and worry filled the air.

"How is it that he thinks *he* can defeat Goliath?

He is only a boy," one soldier said to his friend, "and a very young one, at that."

"There is so much at stake," said another, despairing. "If he fails, we will be slaves to the Philistines. I could not bear such a fate!"

David and the soldiers passed in front of Ethan's tent. The young shepherd, head held high, seemed so calm; it was hard to believe he was headed for what seemed certain death.

"Where are they going?" Samuel asked, watching David and the soldiers disappear around a corner.

"I heard them say that David had been summoned by King Saul," Katie answered.

"Come on! Let's follow them!" Peter jumped up. "I want to see Saul's face when he realizes that David is just a boy. A boy like me."

Peter was already out of sight before Ethan could protest. "I guess we'd better hurry if we want to catch up to him," he said, shrugging his shoulders.

Saul stood anxiously at the door of his tent, awaiting the shepherd boy's arrival. The prospect of being rid of Goliath had lifted his dark spirits, but when David finally arrived, Saul's hopes seemed to fade away. Saul knew David as the son of Jesse who had once healed his spirit with his harp playing, but now David stood before him as the only one willing to confront Goliath. He was so young! And so small!

Ethan and the children caught up with Peter, who watched from the edge of the enclosure around the king's tent. Peter beckoned for the others to join him. Quietly, they made their way to his side. There, they could see and hear all that transpired.

"Your Majesty, here is the shepherd you sent for," the soldiers said, presenting David to the king. David approached Saul and bowed low before him.

"Is what I have been told true?" Saul asked David.

Respectfully referring to himself as "thy servant," David repeated his intention to face Goliath. "Let no man's heart fail because of him; thy servant will go and fight with this Philistine."

Saul answered David's heartfelt declaration with doubt and fear: "Thou art not able to go against this Philistine to fight with him: for thou art but a youth, and he a man of war from his youth."

David considered Saul's concern for a moment before answering, "Thy servant kept his father's sheep, and there came a lion, and a bear, and took a lamb out of the flock: and I went out after him, and smote him, and delivered it out of his mouth: and when he arose against me, I caught him by his beard, and smote him, and slew him."

"Did you know that?" Matthew whispered to Samuel.

"I had heard the story, but I didn't think it could be true. A lion and a bear? That's incredible!" Samuel sputtered.

David went on, speaking with both confidence and humility, "Thy servant slew both the lion and the bear: and this . . . Philistine shall be as one of them, seeing he hath defied the armies of the living God. The Lord that delivered me out of the paw of the lion, and out of the paw of the bear, he will deliver me out of the hand of this Philistine."

Saul looked on David, filled with admiration for David's desire to deliver his people and to serve

his God. "Go, and the Lord be with thee," Saul said, pronouncing his blessing on David's plan.

"He's really going to do it!" Susannah was in awe. "I thought maybe Saul would forbid it."

"I think David's faith in God has given Saul hope—hope that a young boy can bring down a giant," Katie said, deeply touched by the courage of the shepherd boy.

Saul called for his armor. He placed his own heavy coat of mail over David's young shoulders and his brass helmet onto David's head. Then he gave his sword to David to fasten at his side.

"David does not look at ease in that armor," Ethan said, voicing everyone's thoughts.

"If he has God on his side, why does he need armor anyway?" Peter asked.

"Well," Katie reminded him, "Mom says we can count on God's help only when we've first done everything we can to help ourselves." Then she looked over at David, who was struggling to move in Saul's armor. "But it looks like wearing that heavy armor may hinder his fighting more than it will help."

That must have been exactly what David was

thinking, because he removed the heavy brass helmet and the mail and gave it all back to King Saul's servant.

He turned to the king and said, "I cannot go with these; for I have not proved them. God will deliver me out of the hand of the Philistine."

"Go, and the Lord be with thee," Saul repeated.

David took his staff in hand and secured his sling on his belt. Then he strode with determination through the camp to meet Goliath, leaving Saul at the door of his tent, wishing that his trust in God was as sure as young David's.

Chapter Nine

For the Battle Is the Lord's

The shadows lengthened in the afternoon sun. David, without armor or heavy weapons, walked the path that dropped off the ridge of the foothills, down into the valley of Elah below. The Israelite army came out in force to watch the young shepherd contend with the giant. Although his victory seemed improbable, David's determination to fight Goliath had breathed new life into the Israelite army, and the soldiers rallied in fierce support of the shepherd boy.

Ethan and the children watched from the ridge as David descended into the valley.

"He looks so small, and Goliath looks so big," Peter lamented. And then he brightened. "I just have to remember that the Lord is on David's side, and that makes all the difference."

"That's right, Peter. Remember, David trusts God completely, or he never would attempt to defeat a warrior three times his size!" Susannah said. And then she reminded the children of the words of the song they had learned from David: "'Our God defends all those who love and trust Him.' And surely I have never seen such trust as I see in David!" she concluded.

When David reached the valley floor, he stopped at the stream and picked up five smooth stones. These he placed in his shepherd's bag. He secured his sling in his right hand, crossed the stream, and approached the Philistine.

Goliath, led by his shield bearer, swaggered confidently to meet David. His eyes were filled with disgust for the insolent young shepherd who dared to challenge him.

"Am I a dog, that thou comest to me with a staff?" Goliath roared. "Come to me," he taunted David, "and I will give thy flesh unto the fowls of the air, and to the beasts of the field!"

Katie was frightened by Goliath's menacing words. "Oh no, now what?" She moaned softly.

"Come on, Sis." Matthew tried to calm her fear. "Where is your faith?"

"It's here in my heart, I promise," she said. "I just didn't know I'd need so much of it."

David stood his ground, unshaken by Goliath's vicious threats. He stepped forward and addressed Goliath in a loud, steady voice. "Thou comest to me with a sword, and with a spear, and with a shield," he said, acknowledging the shield bearer who stood between him and Goliath. "But I come to thee in the name of the Lord of hosts, the God of the armies of Israel, whom thou hast defied."

"David doesn't even seem afraid," Peter breathed in wonder.

"That is because he knows he has God on his side," Ethan replied.

"It's like having an invisible shield bearer to always protect you," Peter remarked.

Then David spoke again, sounding even more certain and assured. "This day will the Lord deliver thee into mine hand; and I will smite thee, and take thine head from thee; and I will give the carcasses of the host of the Philistines this day unto the fowls of the air, and to the wild beasts of the earth."

Goliath, still unfazed by David's words, scoffed at the warnings of the small shepherd. But gaining strength in the Lord with each passing moment, David then declared that all this would come to pass so "that all the earth may know that there is a God in Israel. And all this assembly," he said pointing to the two opposing armies gathered on either side of the valley, "shall know that the Lord saveth not with sword and spear: for the battle is the Lord's, and he will give you into our hands."

Tiring of David's persistent show of confidence, Goliath started toward him.

David did not shrink from the advancing giant. As he ran toward Goliath, he put his hand in his bag and deftly removed one of his five smooth stones. In one practiced motion, he tucked the stone securely into his sling. He swung the small apparatus in wide circles above his head, momentum building with each pass. As he had so many times before, he judged just the right moment to

release the stone, and he sent it hurtling through the air toward its intended target.

David's aim was sure. The stone found its mark, sinking like a bullet into the small area of Goliath's forehead not protected by his thick helmet. The massive giant pitched forward, falling hard to the earth on his face.

David ran to the motionless Goliath and stood on top of him. He drew his sword out of its sheath, and he cut off Goliath's head.

"Oh no!" Katie buried her head in Matthew's back.

The color drained from Susannah's face, and she, too, turned away from the dreadful scene.

In no time, pandemonium broke out in both camps. Fear gripped the Philistine army when they saw that their champion was dead. With Goliath gone, there was nothing to keep the Israelite army from attacking. Instinctively, when the Israelites sensed their advantage, a shout went up from the troops, and they swarmed like ants down the mountain to the valley floor below, Ethan among them, in hot pursuit of the retreating Philistine army.

"Whoa! This is intense! I've never been this close to a battle before!" Peter exhaled loudly, standing on the deserted mountain ridge.

Matthew rolled his eyes. "I think you mean you've never been *anywhere* near a battle before, little brother," he murmured with a smile.

"Samuel, I think we had better start for home, so we arrive before dark," Susannah said, checking the position of the sun in the sky. "We will need to tell Mother and Father that Ethan is safe, and that the Philistine army has been defeated. And better than that, we can tell them that he will be home soon."

"That will make Mother very happy," Samuel beamed.

"Me too!" Susannah exulted. She adored her older brother, and she couldn't wait to have him home again.

"I guess we had better be getting home too," Matthew said reluctantly.

The twins escorted their new friends to the edge of the camp and bid them farewell.

"Matthew, Peter, and Katie, it was a pleasure

to meet you. I hope our paths will cross again," Samuel said.

"I hope so too," Matthew replied sincerely, waving good-bye.

"We are going this way," Susannah said, as she pointed across the field behind the encampment. "Will you walk with us?"

"Uh . . . well . . . we better take the shortcut that goes this other way, or we might be late," Katie said, thinking quickly.

"Good-bye, then, friends. Until we meet again," Susannah said. And the latter-day children embraced the children from ancient times.

"Until we meet again," Katie said softly as she and her brothers headed over the brow of the hill.

Chapter Ten

Five Ideas, Five Smooth Stones

Under the shade of same Elah tree that had wel-
comed them that very morning, Katie, Matthew,
and Peter joined hands for the journey home. The
air swirled around them, scooping them up and off
the ground. When they were high above the valley, Katie opened her eyes. For just a moment, she
thought she could see Samuel and Susannah making their way down the backside of the mountain.

The next thing she knew, she felt soft pillows
cushion her body as she arrived safely in Grandma's
art cottage. Matthew and Peter settled into the
pillows next to Katie, and they greeted her with
knowing winks and brotherly smiles.

Grandma, as always, sat in her rocking chair
reading aloud from her scriptures, seemingly

unaware that the children were ever gone, or that they had returned.

"So David prevailed over the Philistine with a sling and with a stone, and smote the Philistine and slew him; but there was no sword in the hand of David."

Before she could say another word, Peter jumped up to examine the painting. The armies, ready for battle, stood lifeless and still on the canvas. Goliath, the giant Philistine, outfitted with armor and spears, waited for David's approach.

David, dressed only in a simple tunic, stood with his sling, ready to challenge Goliath.

"I never realized how small David was compared to Goliath, until I saw them both in person," Peter said, as he studied the painting.

"You saw them in person? Oh my, Peter, what an imagination you have!" Grandma chuckled.

"It wasn't my imagination," Peter said matter-of-factly. "I really saw them."

"I think you mean that you really saw them in your mind's eye, isn't that right, buddy?" Matthew cleared his throat loudly.

"Uh . . ." Peter realized his mistake. "Right, Matthew. In my mind's eye."

"Well, since you 'really' saw David and Goliath, what did you learn from them?" Grandma asked.

"Well," Peter ventured, "David had a huge, and boy, do I mean *huge*, problem named Goliath."

"Yes, Goliath was an enormous problem, wasn't he?" Grandma agreed.

"Goliath was so big that no one had the courage to fight him. They were all cowards. Even the king," Peter said.

"So how is it that David, just a young boy, had the courage to fight a giant?" Grandma asked the question slowly, emphasizing its importance.

"It wasn't just courage, Grandma," Peter explained. "He had courage, mixed with a whole lot of faith in Heavenly Father."

"And how did he exercise that faith?"

This time Matthew answered. "The Philistines had declared war on Israel and Israel's God. It wasn't just about winning the battle, Grandma. It was about defending Israel's honor. David had faith that God would help him if he fought in His name."

"Exactly," Grandma said. "In fact, David wrote a song about that."

The children froze. "He did?" Katie finally asked, wondering how Grandma could possibly know about the song the twins sang to them in the valley of Elah in ancient Palestine.

"Oh, yes, David wrote lots of songs. We call them the Psalms of the Old Testament." Grandma quickly flipped the pages of her Bible. "In the fifth Psalm, David says, 'But let all those that put their trust in thee rejoice: let them ever shout for joy, because thou defendest them: let them also that love thy name be joyful in thee.'"

The children looked at each other, relieved to learn how Grandma knew about David's song. Grandma went on, "When you read those Psalms, you start to understand how much David loved Heavenly Father, and that he knew Him well. Then it's not so surprising that he believed that he could defeat Goliath. He knew God would help him."

"King Saul sure didn't think David could do it. He told David 'thou art but a youth,'" Katie said.

"But David proved him wrong. I guess just

because you're young, it doesn't mean you can't do great things," Matthew said thoughtfully.

"And guess what else, Grandma?" Peter jumped in. "David had so much faith, he wouldn't even wear the king's armor to protect him. He decided to use his little old homemade slingshot."

"That took a lot of faith, didn't it?" Grandma agreed, enjoying the lively discussion.

"I don't think David got that kind of faith all of a sudden, though," Katie observed. "He had been protected by the Lord before. He fought off a bear and a lion that attacked his flock. And he killed that lion bare-handed! So maybe facing Goliath, as long as he had God's help, didn't seem so impossible to him."

"Here's a question for you. In this story, Goliath was a person, but sometimes other things may seem like a Goliath to us. What are the Goliaths we face in our lives?" Grandma asked, with her eyes lingering last on Peter.

"I know just what you're getting at, Grandma," Peter answered her.

"Really? Do you have some Goliaths in your

life, Peter?" Grandma asked innocently, but she already knew what his answer would be.

"I sure do! Math!" he said, his frustration mounting at the mere thought of the subject.

"So, math is your Goliath," Matthew confirmed.

Peter nodded glumly. "But I'm not like David."

"That's not true," Katie consoled him. "I'd say you're a lot like David."

"How?" Peter asked.

"First of all, you believe in God, don't you?"

"Absolutely!" he answered with all the conviction he could muster.

"Okay, then, if you believe in Him, you know you can rely on Him for help, right?" Matthew pressed.

"I suppose so," Peter replied, starting to feel like there might be some hope for him with his Goliath.

"And you're a man of action, just like David," Matthew went on. "I've seen you do brave things to help others lots of times. Remember when you rescued the neighbor's cat from the tree when no one else dared climb it?"

"What we need is a strategy for conquering your Goliath, in this case known as math," Katie giggled as she slipped her arm around her brother.

From her rocking chair, Grandma offered the first suggestion. "Here's one idea, honey: Say a prayer before you face the giant. Then you can feel certain you have Heavenly Father's help."

"Here's another, bro," Matthew chimed in. "Katie and I could help you with your homework every night. Practice makes perfect, you know."

"Thanks, I'd like that," Peter said gratefully. "And I was thinking maybe I could ask the teacher for extra time to finish my tests."

"Good idea," Katie encouraged him.

"I could also try really hard to pay close attention in class. Sometimes I struggle with that," Peter admitted.

"And always do your very best," Matthew sounded like he was speaking from experience. "When you're busy doing your best, there's no time to feel discouraged."

"You know, each of these ideas is like one of the five smooth stones that David collected from the brook before he went out to meet his Goliath,"

Grandma pointed out. "He didn't know how many he would need, but he was prepared to use all of them."

"And that's how he showed his faith, isn't it, Grandma?" Peter said, getting the idea. "So here's what I'm going to do: I'm going to pray, get help, talk to my teacher, pay attention, and do my best. Five ideas, five smooth stones. Better watch out, math. I'm going to meet you head on!"

Peter took one last look at the painting of David, the shepherd boy, facing the Philistine giant, Goliath. As he shifted for a better look, he felt something in the front pocket of his jeans. Slowly he reached in . . . and pulled out one of the stones he had collected that very morning at the pond! A giant-sized smile of optimism and courage crept across young Peter's face, as his fingers closed around the smooth little rock.

About the Authors

Alice W. Johnson, a published author and composer, is a featured speaker for youth groups, adult firesides, and women's seminars. After receiving a B.A. in economics from Brigham Young University and serving a mission to Taiwan, Alice was an executive in a worldwide strategy consulting company, and then in a leadership training firm. She is now a homemaker living in Eagle, Idaho, with her husband, Paul, and their four young children.

Allison H. Warner gained her early experience living with her family in countries around the world. Returning to the United States as a young woman, she began her vocation as an actress and writer, developing and performing in such productions as *The Farley Family Reunion.* She and her husband, David, reside in Provo, Utah, where they are raising two active boys.

About the Illustrator

Casey Nelson grew up the oldest of eight children in a Navy family, so she moved quite often during her childhood. Graduating with a degree in illustration, she taught figure drawing in the illustration department at Brigham Young University, worked as an artist for video games, and performed in an improvisational comedy troupe. Casey is employed by the Walt Disney Company as a cinematic artist for their video games.